Melody and Rhythm

Melody and Rhythm
Semester 4

Bill Stevens
Director of Musicianship
Santa Clara University
billstevens.net

Avivo
An Avivo Publication
www.avivo.com

Contents

Acknowledgements

Developing the *Melody and Rhythm* curriculum has been a labor of love spanning several years. I have had help from a team of extraordinary people. Foremost, I want to thank my editor, Dr. Loretta Notareschi, whose discerning eye and meticulous attention to detail have been beyond parallel. Her clarity and care have made this a much stronger book.

I have been blessed with two very diligent copy editors: Lydia Davidson and Nicole Yazmin Jacobus. Their capabilities and talents are surpassed in value only by their willingness to dive into any project and learn along the way. (The world is waiting for you two — thank you.)

I would also like to warmly thank my Avivo colleague and mentor Dr. Pam Quist for a lifetime of friendship, for helping me to shape the overall structure of this course, and for many delightful lunches over Thai food.

I have had the great fortune to learn musicianship and sight singing from fantastic models. In particular, I want to thank Patricia Plude and Leo Wanenchak, whose deep love of learning and willingness to pass along the fruits of their learning to other teachers are priceless.

I also want to thank Margaret Simons and Sharon Chu for thorough and insightful proofreading; Phi Lam and Kevin Yee for many hours spent poring through recordings and scores with me; Phi Lam for assistance finding folk melodies; Reilly Farrell for being available as a notation consultant; Chris Nalls for lots of encouragement, feedback, and photo-copying; Leland Kusmer for developing the LaTeX package for this book; Steve Kusmer for designing the cover and title page; Dr. Shawn Crouch for help pacing the harmonic content; Chip Newton for feedback about lead sheet formatting; Dr. Scot Hanna-Weir for suggesting that I include examples with figured bass and harmonic analysis; Michael Howell for assistance navigating the world of contemporary popular music; Hans Boepple and John Kennedy for loaning books and recordings; and members of the Lilypond-Users group for assistance troubleshooting various notation issues.

I want to thank Phyllis Magal and Dr. Lynn Hillberg Jencks for lots of good energy and for helping me talk through many of the decisions that went into this text.

I want to thank the College of Arts and Sciences at Santa Clara University for supporting research for this book with several Dean's Grants.

Lastly, thank you to Carla and Tom Stevens for a lifetime of encouragement and support.

About the Author

Bill Stevens directs the musicianship program at Santa Clara University. He is a founding member of Avivo, a collective of master educators dedicated to cultivating creativity through music teaching, and served on the faculty of The Walden School for twelve years. Bill is the author of *Jazz Musicianship: A Guidebook for Integrated Learning.* He has performed as a guest pianist with The Silkroad Ensemble. Bill is a recipient of the prestigious Presidential Scholars Award and was a Level 1 Finalist with NFAA (now YoungArts) in music composition. Curious about the relationship between creativity, learning, and psychological process, Bill studied psychotherapy with the Helix Training Program and is a certified Somatic Experiencing Practitioner. Learn more at his website: www.billstevens.net.

Introduction

This is the final volume of the *Melody and Rhythm* curriculum, comprising Chapters 19 through 24.

Rhythmically, we will work with advanced tuplets in Chapter 19, explore ways of stretching the bounds of meter in Chapter 21, and introduce metric modulations and advanced polyrhythms in Chapter 23.

Melodically, we are delving into realms of increasing chromaticism. In Chapter 20, we will discover some new scales and modes, exploring different ways of mixing them together. In Chapter 22, we will experiment with even divisions of the octave, working with the whole-tone, hexatonic, and octatonic scales. In Chapter 24, we will abandon all reference to scale and explore freely chromatic melodies.

The structure of Semester 4 will be familiar from previous volumes. Use this structure to spice up your practice. Add dynamics and articulations to the "Interpret" examples. Practice the "Jam Session" examples in a group and take turns improvising solos over the repeating patterns. Use the "Analysis," "Figured Bass," and "Lead Sheet" examples to practice singing bass lines and harmony parts in support of the written melody. Can you tap the top part of a rhythm duet with one hand while you tap the bottom part with your other hand? Can you sing the top part of a melody duet while playing the bottom at the piano?

We are arriving at highly advanced material. My hope is that you can look back over what you have learned during the first three semesters of this course and be inspired by the progress you have made. If you continue to show up consistently, take the step that is in front of you, and trust partial progress, there need be no limit to what you are capable of learning.

Bill Stevens
December 2018
Santa Clara, California

Chapter 19

More Tuplets

We are moving into the territory of advanced rhythm topics. In this chapter, we explore manifold ways of dividing the beat. We will work with tuplet subdivisions in section 1, with quintuplets in section 2, and septuplets in section 3.

19.1   Tuplet Subdivisions

Previously, we have worked with tuplets that fill the space of a single beat, such as three triplet eighth notes in 4/4 time. We have also worked with tuplets that spread across multiple beats, such as triplet quarter notes filling two beats of 4/4 time or four quadruplets filling the space of three beats. In this section, we work with tuplets of shorter duration: tuplets that fill the space of part of a beat.

Be flexible with the use of rhythm syllables here. Study each example. Use ta-tu-te for groups of three and ta-ki-ti-ki for groups of four. Some of these examples have sextuplets: six notes in the space of a beat. Sometimes these are beamed as two groups of three (ta-tu-te ta-tu-te), sometimes as three groups of two (ta-ki tu-ki te-ki).

Sextuplets with Flexible Syllables

Generally, notes under a tuplet bracket are shorter than their non-bracketed counterparts: triplet eighth notes are shorter than regular eighth notes, quadruplet quarters are shorter than regular quarters, etc. An exception to this occurs with even numbered tuplets such as duplets or quadruplets in compound meter. These are generally notated as longer versions of their non-tuplet counterparts. In examples B and F for instance, the duplet eighth notes are longer than the regular eighth notes, sounding like eighths in simple meter. The same is true for the quadruplet sixteenth notes and the octuplet thirty-second notes.

More Tuplets in Compound Meter

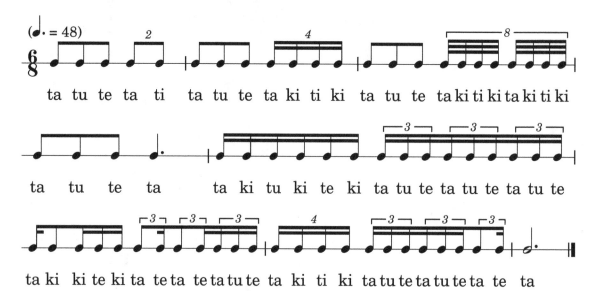

19.1a

19.1c Interpret

Pomposo (♩ = 60)

19.1d Interpret

Bellicoso (♩ = 72)

19.1e

19.1f

19.1g

Espirando (♩ = 60)

19.1h

Pensively ($\textstyle\frac{}{}$ = 48)

19.1i

19.1j

19.2   Quintuplets

We can divide a beat or several beats into five even parts, yielding quintuplets. I prefer to speak quintuplets with the letters a-b-c-d-e.[1]

Notice the flexible use of letters in the vocalise below, where a-b-c-d-e is used for quintuplets filling a single beat as well as for those spread across multiple beats. When quintuplets are spread across two beats, as in the penultimate bar of the vocalise, the a-b-c should be in the first beat and the d-e in the second, with the beat falling precisely between c and d.

Quintuplet Vocalise

19.2a

---

[1]Though it is just as easy to use numbers at this stage, 1-2-3-4-5, we will be working with groupings of seven in the next section and of nine, eleven, and thirteen in Chapter 21. I find that letters are easier than numbers in those situations because of the polysyllabic nature of "seven," "eleven," and "thirteen." I encourage the use of letters here as it will make that later work easier.

19.2b

19.2c Interpret

19.2d Interpret

Volante (♪. = 84)

19.2e

Impending Doom (♩ = 96)

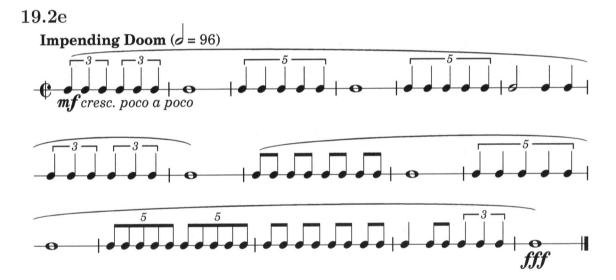

19.2f

19.2g

Energico con fuoco ($\bullet$ = 80)

19.2h

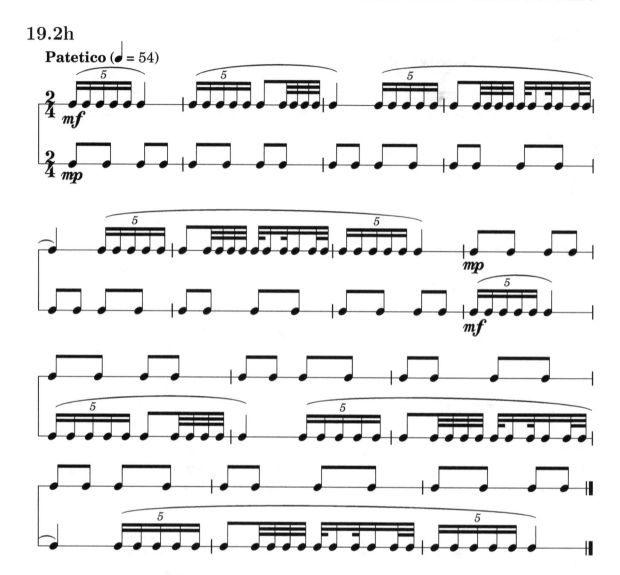

19.2i

Falling rain (♩ = 58)

19.2j

19.3 Septuplets

In this section, we explore dividing the beat into seven parts, forming septuplets. I prefer to speak septuplets with the letters a-b-c-d-e-f-g. As with our work with quintuplets, notice the flexible use of these letters in the vocalise below. When septuplets are spread across two beats, the a-b-c-d fall in the first beat and the e-f-g in the second, with the beat falling precisely between the d and the e.

Septuplet Vocalise

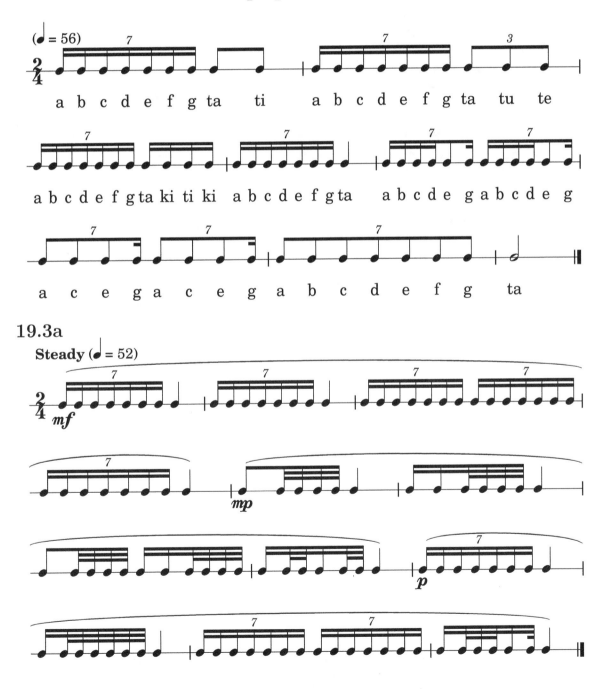

19.3a

19.3b

Heavy and plodding (♩ = 46)

19.3c Interpret

Winding and unwinding (♩ = 60)

19.3d Interpret

19.3e

19.3g

19.3h

Sospirando (♩ = 40)

19.3i

19.3j

Hail Storm (♩ = 52)

Chapter 20

Modal Chromaticism

In Chapter 18, we defined a mode as a reorientation of an existing scale around a new center pitch. In this chapter, we will continue to work with the concept of mode, discovering some new scales and combining familiar scales in new ways. We are moving toward highly chromatic territory in Chapter 22 and Chapter 24. In this chapter, we will use further work with modes as a bridge toward increasing chromaticism.

In section 1, we will work with minor and major modes of the blues scale. In section 2, we will spend time with some less common scales such as Locrian (the seventh mode of major) and Lydian-dominant (the fourth mode of melodic minor). In section 3, we will explore changing modes while preserving the same tonic. In section 4, we will explore changing modes while moving the tonic.

I use a series of warm up exercises when I am teaching this material. Treating C as do throughout and using chromatic syllables where appropriate, we sing half and whole steps in all sounding transpositions as modeled below. Notice the enharmonic spellings in several places for extra practice with chromatic syllables.[1]

---

[1]I also use descending forms of the same exercises.

Half Steps and Whole Steps Vocalise

Once a class is comfortable singing half steps and whole steps in this way, we move on to stepwise trichords:

Stepwise Trichords Vocalise

After trichords, we work with tetrachords, pentachords, and hexachords before singing entire scales in all twelve sounding transpositions. Though I continue to use movable do when teaching modal chromaticism, these warm up activities are invaluable preparation for moving to fixed do with chromatic syllables in Chapter 22 and Chapter 24.

20.1 The Blues Scale

Take the Aeolian scale (natural minor) on A. Now, remove the second and sixth scale degrees, yielding a scale with five notes per octave. Just as a pentagon has five sides, this five note scale is the pentatonic scale.[2] Notice that there are no half steps or tritones, the most dissonant intervals, in the pentatonic scale.

Now, we will add a single chromatic tone between the perfect fourth and perfect fifth. The resulting scale is known as the blues scale. Notice that the chromatic tone is spelled as an augmented fourth above the tonic when ascending and as a diminished fifth when descending; this change in spelling is common though not essential.

---

[2]To be more specific, it is the minor pentatonic scale; notice the minor triad on its tonic: A-C-E.

Discovering the Blues Scale

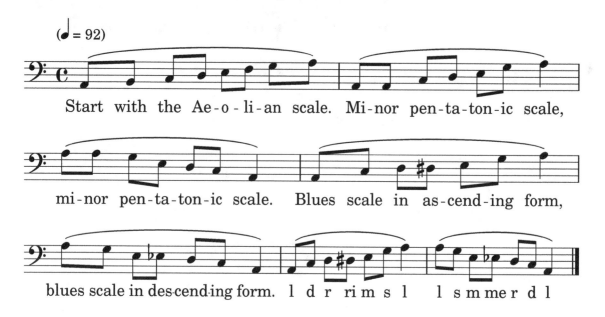

The Blues Scale in the Parallel Minor Key

Examples A through D feature the blues scale written in the parallel minor key. The only accidental in the scale is the tritone, which is sometimes written as an augmented fourth above the tonic and sometimes as a diminished fifth. The symbol on beat three of bar eight in example C is a fall off, indicating a glissando downward at the end of the note.

20.1a

20.1b

20.1c

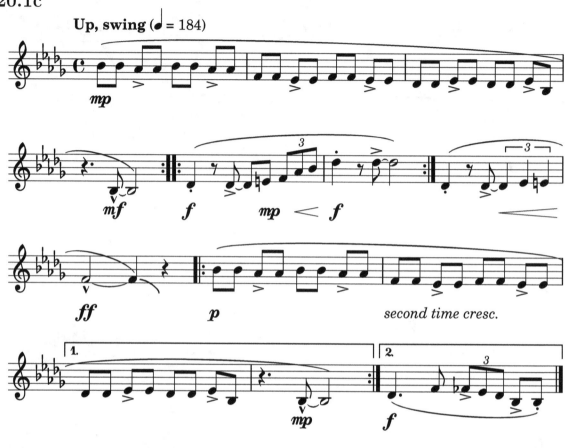

20.1d

The Blues Major Scale

The blues scale contains two minor triads and one major triad. Can you find them? Notice that this configuration of triads encompasses both the relative major/minor and the parallel major/minor relationships.

Relationship of Triads in the Blues Scale

Re - la - tive mi - nor, re - la - tive ma - jor, pa - ra - llel mi - nor.

Consider just the relative major/minor triads for a moment. We can think of the blues scale as a kind of minor scale, in light of the minor triad on its tonic. If we reorganize the blues scale around the root of the major triad, we find a major mode of the blues scale, sometimes called the blues major scale, or the major blues scale. Examples E through H feature this major mode of the blues scale written in the parallel major key. The chromatic passing tone in the scale now falls between the major second and major third.

The Major Mode of the Blues Scale

d m s s m d   d r r i m s l d   d l s m m er d

20.1e

20.1f

20.1g

20.1h

The Blues Scale in the Parallel Major Key

Examples I through M feature the blues scale written in the parallel major key. This is fairly common, in spite of the minor sound of the scale, as the blues scale is often used over harmonies with a major third (like the major-minor seventh chord). Here, the minor third, tritone, and minor seventh of the scale, known as "blue notes," are all written with accidentals.

The Blues Scale in the Parallel Major Key

20.1i

20.1j

20.1k

20.1l

20.1m

Specialty Examples

20.1n Duet

20.1o Jam Session

Cool (♩· = 108)

20.1p Analysis

20.1q Figured Bass

Ballad, sixteenths swung ($\flat$ = 58)

20.1r Lead Sheet

20.1s Find the Music

20.1t Fill in the Blanks

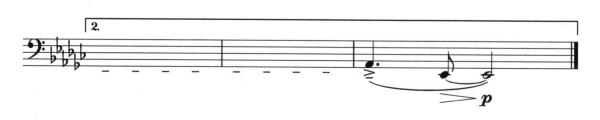

Listening Examples

- Jazz: Clifford Brown, "Swingin'," from *Study in Brown* (0:00–0:07).

- Soul: Aretha Franklin, "Niki Hoeky," from *Lady Soul*, written by James Ford, Lolly Vegas, and Pat Vegas. Notice the expressivity in the vocal line.

- Soul: Aretha Franklin, "Good to Me as I Am to You," from *Lady Soul*, written by Aretha Franklin and Ted White.

- Gospel: Patty Griffin, "Move Up," from *Downtown Church*. This is a great arrangement of a traditional song.

- Folk Jazz: Joni Mitchell, "The Hissing of Summer Lawns," from *The Hissing of Summer Lawns* (0:13–0:39), written by Joni Mitchell and John Guerin.

- New Soul: Amy Winehouse, "Rehab," from *Back to Black* (0:00–0:33).

20.2 More Modes and Scales

In this section, we introduce some other modes/scales that are occasionally used, working with Locrian, Lydian-dominant, and various modes of harmonic and melodic minor.

The Locrian Scale

There was one mode of the major scale, the seventh, that we did not cover in Chapter 18. This is the Locrian scale/mode.

The Seventh Mode of the Major Scale

It is the least commonly used of all of the modes of the major scale because it has a diminished rather than a perfect fifth above the tonic. The tonic triad in Locrian is diminished, and is therefore very unstable.

Unstable Tonic Triad

Locrian is like natural minor with lowered second and fifth scale degrees.

Natural Minor and Locrian

Notice that Locrian also resembles the blues scale. Both scales have a minor third, perfect fourth, diminished fifth, and minor seventh.

Locrian and the Blues Scale

Examples A and B present Locrian written in the major key a half step above the tonic. Example C presents Locrian in the parallel minor key, with lowered second and fifth degrees. Example D presents Locrian in the parallel major key, with lowered second, third, fifth, sixth, and seventh degrees.

20.2a

20.2b

Haru no uta

Anonymous

20.2c

20.2d

The Lydian-Dominant Scale

Begin with the ascending form of melodic minor. Now, find its fourth mode. This is a scale commonly used in jazz and contemporary music. The first six notes of this scale resemble the Lydian mode. This scale also has a dominant seventh chord on its tonic. Consequently, it is known as the Lydian-dominant scale.

The Lydian-Dominant Scale

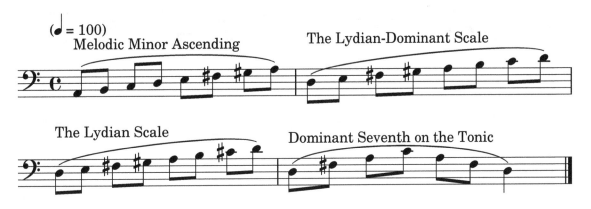

Examples E and F present the Lydian-dominant scale in the parallel major key, with raised fourth and lowered seventh degrees. Example G presents B Lydian-dominant in the context of F♯ major, emphasizing its relationship to the Lydian mode. (Notice that the third degree of F♯ major is lowered to create the "dominant" sound.) Example H presents D Lydian-dominant in the context of G major. Here, G♯s are used for the raised fourth of the Lydian sound. For reference, I have written out the scale used in each of these examples. Before practicing each example, take some time to warm up with the scale.

Scale for Example E

20.2e

Scale for Example F

20.2f

La Mer - No. 1, De l'aube à midi sur la mer

Claude Debussy

Scale for Example G

20.2g

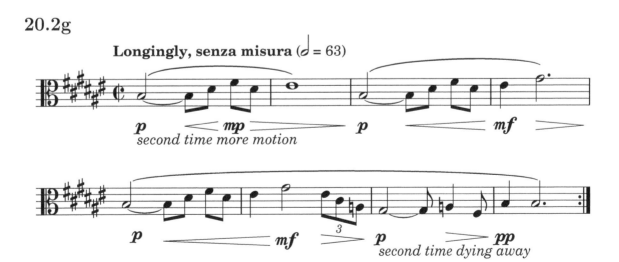

Scale for Example H

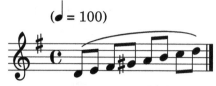

20.2h

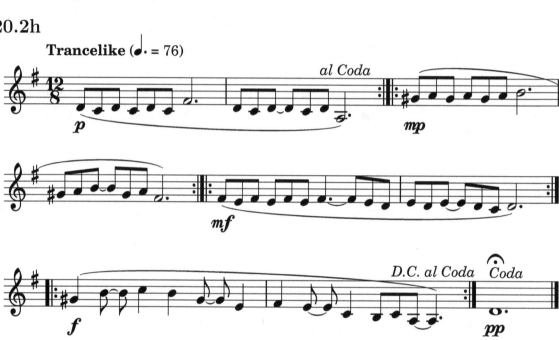

Other Scales

Examples I through M feature other scales. Orient to each example. Notice if each degree is raised, lowered, or falls naturally within the key signature. Write out the scale for each example as I did earlier with examples E through H. Map out the steps of the scale: which are half, which whole, and which augmented? Practice singing up and down the scale carefully. Then explore the melody.

20.2i

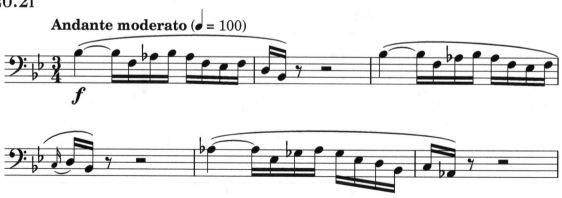

20.2j

20.2l

20.2m

Specialty Examples

20.2n Canon

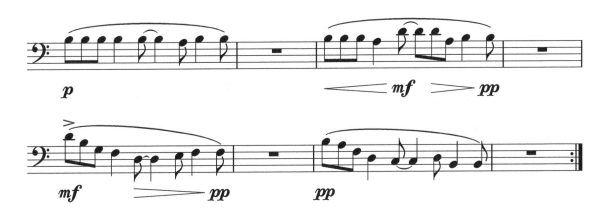

20.2o Jam Session

Laid back (♩. = 92)

Loop indefinitely

Cadence

20.2p Analysis

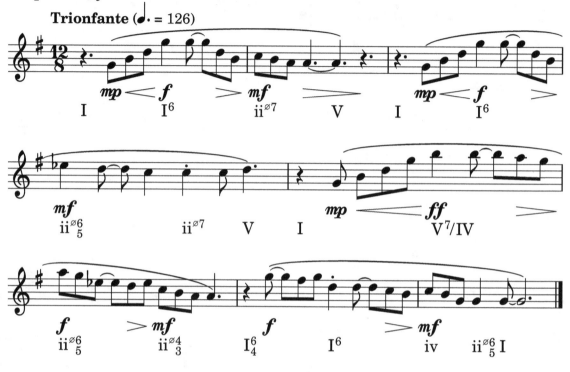

20.2q Figured Bass

20.2r Lead Sheet

20.2s Find the Music

20.2t Fill in the Blanks

Listening Examples

- Classical: Béla Bartók, *Mikrokosmos* Vol. I No. 10, "With Alternate Hands."

- Classical: Béla Bartók, *Mikrokosmos* Vol. I No. 29, "Imitation Reflected."

- Classical: Béla Bartók, *Mikrokosmos* Vol. II No. 41, "Melody with Accompaniment."

- Classical: Béla Bartók, *Mikrokosmos* Vol. II No. 58, "In Oriental Style." Though the final cadance implies D harmonic minor, most of this example sounds like it is in the fourth mode of harmonic minor (built on G).

- Classical: Béla Bartók, *Mikrokosmos* Vol. II No. 63, "Buzzing." This is a great example of the Locrian mode.

- Television: Danny Elfman, theme from *The Simpsons*. This theme makes ample use of the Lydian-dominant scale in multiple transpositions.

- Jazz Fusion: Pat Metheny Group, "The Heat of the Day," from *Imaginary Day* (0:08–0:45), written by Pat Metheny and Lyle Mays.

- Alternative Country: Neko Case, "Outro with Bees," from *Blacklisted* (0:00–0:17). Follow the instrumental melody.

20.3   Mixing Modes, Preserving the Tonic

In 14.1, we explored the parallel major/minor relationship, changing between the Ionian and Aeolian modes while preserving the same tonic. In this section, we will do much the same thing, changing between different scales/modes while preserving the same tonic. Only here, we will work with scales other than just major (Ionian) and minor (Aeolian).

Examples in the Parallel Major Key

20.3a

Columba aspexit

Hildegard von Bingen

20.3b

20.3c

20.3d

Nocturnes - No. 1, Nuages

Claude Debussy

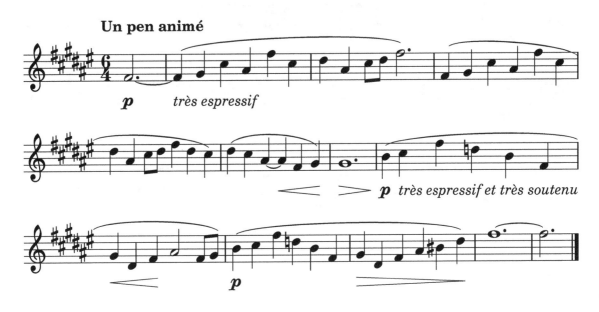

Examples in the Parallel Minor Key

20.3e

Blow Your Trumpet, Gabriel.

Anonymous

20.3f

O Willow, Willow!

Melody from Thomas Tallis's Lute Book

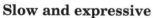

20.3g

Trio for Piano, Violin and Cello - No. 3, Allegro vigoroso

Rebecca Clarke

20.3h

Mixed Examples

20.3i

Theme and Variations for Flute and String Quartet, Op. 80

Amy Beach

20.3j

20.3k

Three Moods of the Sea - No. 1, Requies.

Ethel Smyth

20.3l

20.3m

Peer Gynt Suite No. 2 - The Abduction (Ingrid's Lament)

Edvard Grieg

Specialty Examples

20.3n Duet

Ecco la primavera

Francesco Landini

20.3o Jam Session

This next example features a key change from flats to sharps. Like all of the examples in this section, the tonic does not change, though it looks different on the staff before and after the key change. All of the roman numerals are in reference to D♭/C♯ as the tonic.

20.3p Analysis

20.3q Figured Bass

20.3r Lead Sheet

20.3s Find the Music

20.3t Fill in the Blanks

Listening Examples

- Classical: Béla Bartók, *Mikrokosmos* Vol. I No. 15, "Village Song."

- Classical: Béla Bartók, *Mikrokosmos* Vol. I No. 33, "Slow Dance."

- Classical: Béla Bartók, *Mikrokosmos* Vol. I No. 36, "Free Canon."

- Classical: Béla Bartók, *Mikrokosmos* Vol. II No. 52, "Unison Divided."

- Television: Lalo Schifrin, theme from *Mission: Impossible.*

- Pop Rock: The Turtles, "Happy Together," from *Happy Together*, written by Alan Gordon and Garry Bonner.

- Pop: Joni Mitchell, "Help Me," from *Court and Spark.*

- Folk Jazz: Joni Mitchell, "The Jungle Line," from *The Hissing of Summer Lawns.*

- Country: Dolly Parton, "Early Morning Breeze," from *Jolene*.

- Video Games: Koji Kondo, "Legend of Zelda Suite," performed by The London Philharmonic Orchestra, from *The Greatest Video Game Music* (0:28–1:11). Follow the melody in the violins.

- Folk Rock: 10,000 Maniacs, "Gold Rush Brides," from *Our Time in Eden*, written by Robert Buck and Natalie Merchant. This tune mixes major and Mixolydian.

- Folk Jazz: Joni Mitchell, "Last Chance Lost," from *Turbulent Indigo*.

- Jazz: Michael Brecker, "Tumbleweed," from *Pilgrimage*.

- Video Games: Yasunori Mitsuda, "Chrono Trigger: Main Theme," performed by The London Philharmonic Orchestra, from *The Greatest Video Game Music 2* (0:32–1:02). Follow the theme in the winds.

20.4   Mixing Modes, Moving the Tonic

We have defined parallel major/minor as the major and minor keys that share the same tonic and relative major/minor as the major and minor keys that share the same key signature. Let us consider, for a moment, applying these terms more broadly, thinking of parallel modes as having the same tonic and relative modes as having the same key signature. We could thus speak of C Lydian as the parallel Lydian of C major as both scales have C as the tonic. Likewise, F Lydian would be the relative Lydian of C major as both scales have no sharps or flats.

We can use these broader definitions of relative and parallel to explore ways of connecting distantly related key areas. Consider each of the following examples:

- Begin with C major. Move to the relative Dorian (D Dorian). Now, move to the parallel Major (D major). We can thus think of D major as the parallel major of the relative Dorian of C major.

- Begin with C major. Move to the parallel Phrygian: C Phrygian, which has four flats. Now, move to the relative major of C Phrygian: A♭ major, which also has four flats. We can thus think of A♭ major as the relative major of the parallel Phrygian of C major.

- Begin with C major. Move to the relative Locrian: B Locrian. Now, move to the parallel major of B Locrian: B major. We can thus think of B major as the parallel major of the relative Locrian of C major.

In this section, we explore these kinds of relationships: changing mode and changing tonic; changing the scale while moving the center pitch.

Simple Pivots

Examples A through D pivot between two different key areas. Each key is clearly established and the transition between them is distinct and clean. I have marked each transition point with a "Pivot" indication. If you are using movable do, I recommend moving the do at each pivot point.

20.4a

Piano Quintet No. 2, Op. 31

Louise Farrenc

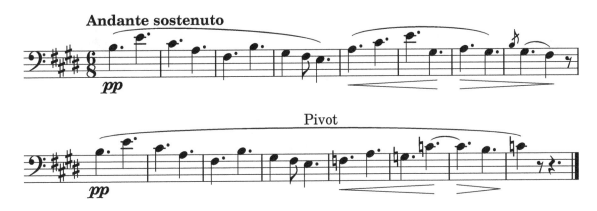

20.4b

Pictures at an Exhibition - Promenade

Modest Mussorgsky

20.4c

Symphony No. 7 in A major, Op. 92 - No. 3, Presto

Ludwig van Beethoven

20.4d

Freely Mixing Two Scales

Examples E through H also each have two scales and two tonics. Unlike the simple pivots above, though, these examples mix their key areas more freely. Example E alternates between C minor and F major. Example F is mostly in D♭ major, with a brief allusion to D major. Example G mixes D harmonic minor and D harmonic major[3] while moving the tonic from D to A. Example H mixes D minor and F minor. I do not recommend moving the do for these examples.

20.4e

Durwan's Song

Anonymous

---

[3]Think of harmonic major as harmonic minor with a major third.

20.4f

Nocturnes, Op. 9 - No. 1, Larghetto in B-flat minor

Frédéric Chopin

20.4g

Charki Hidjaz

Anonymous

20.4h

Symphony No. 3 in D minor

Anton Bruckner

Mixing More Scales

These examples combine three or more different key areas, sometimes pivoting between them definitively and sometimes mixing them more freely. Study each example carefully and decide for yourself how best to approach it.

20.4i

Symphony No. 8 in G major, Op. 88 - Mvt. II, Adagio

Antonín Dvořák

20.4j

Lohengrin, WWV 75 - Act III, Bridal Chorus

Richard Wagner

20.4k

Peer Gynt Suite No. 2, Op. 55 - Arabian Dance

Edvard Grieg

20.4l

Symphony No. 2 in C minor

Anton Bruckner

20.4m

Verschwiegene Liebe

Hugo Wolf

Specialty Examples

20.4n Duet

Aida - Overture

Giuseppe Verdi

20.4o Jam Session

20.4p Analysis

20.4q Figured Bass

20.4r Lead Sheet

20.4s Find the Music

20.4t Fill in the Blanks

Listening Examples

- Classical: Béla Bartók, *Mikrokosmos* Vol. II No. 49, "Crescendo-Diminuendo."

- Classical: Béla Bartók, *Mikrokosmos* Vol. II No. 57, "Accents."

- Classical: Béla Bartók, *Mikrokosmos* Vol. II No. 61, "Pentatonic Melody." Though the melody itself is pentatonic, the accompaniment gives it a modal context.

- Classical: Béla Bartók, *Mikrokosmos* Vol. IV No. 104, "Wandering Through the Keys."

- Television: David Kahn, Melvyn Leonard, and Mort Greene, theme from *Leave it to Beaver (The Toy Parade)*. Follow the tonal shifts between F major and G major.

- Television: Eliot Daniel, theme from *I Love Lucy*.

- Television: William Loose and John Seely, theme from *Dennis the Menace*.

- Television: Sherwood Schwartz and George Wyle, theme from *Gilligan's Island*.

- Bossa Nova: Astrud Gilberto, "The Girl from Ipanema," from *Getz-Gilberto* (1:21–2:34), written by Antônio Carlos Jobim, Vinicius de Moraes, and Norman Gimbel.

- Jazz: Herbie Hancock, "Maiden Voyage," from *Maiden Voyage*.

- Jazz: McCoy Tyner, "Passion Dance," from *The Real McCoy* (0:00–1:09).

- Musical Theater: Harvey Schmidt and Tom Jones, "Try to Remember," from *The Fantasticks* (original cast recording, 0:55–1:51).

- Musical Theater: Charles Strouse and Lee Adams, "A Lot of Livin' to Do," from *Bye Bye Birdie* (original cast recording, 0:04–1:08).

- Folk: Joni Mitchell, "Roses Blue," from *Clouds*.

- Folk: Joni Mitchell, "My Old Man," from *Blue*.

- Alternative Rock: Alanis Morissette, "Head Over Feet," from *Jagged Little Pill*, written by Alanis Morissette and Glen Ballard.

- Hip Hop: Lauryn Hill, "Superstar," from *The Miseducation of Lauryn Hill*, written by Lauryn Hill and James Poyser.

- Jazz: Michael Brecker, "Itsbynne Reel," from *Don't Try This at Home*, head by Michael Brecker and Don Grolnick. Check out the modal shift at the 2:12 mark.

- Video Games: Charlotte Martin, Michael Richard Plowman, and Tommy Tallarico, "Advent Rising: Muse," performed by The London Philharmonic Orchestra, from *The Greatest Video Game Music* (2:21–3:43). Follow the melody from the piano to the brass, to the double reeds, and back to the brass again.

- Video Games: Kenji Yamamoto, "Super Metroid: A Symphonic Poem," performed by The London Philharmonic Orchestra, from *The Greatest Video Game Music 2* (0:02–0:23).

- Video Games: Christopher Lennertz, "Mass Effect 3: A Future for the Krogan," performed by The London Philharmonic Orchestra, from *The Greatest Video Game Music 2* (0:26–1:04). Follow the vocal line in relationship to the root of each chord. The tonal center changes quickly and often.

Chapter 21

Stretching the Bounds of Meter

Over the past few rhythm chapters, we have been expanding the realm of possibilities with respect to meter. In Chapter 15, we worked with changing meters, making the downbeat less predictable. In Chapter 17, we worked with odd and composite meters, making the organization of beats within the meter less predictable. In Chapter 19, we worked with more tuplets, making the division and/or subdivision of the beat less predictable.

There are more ways, though, to stretch the bounds of meter. What about tuplet groupings of nine, eleven, thirteen, or fifteen notes? What about polyphonic music where each part is in a different meter? What about musical passages that use no meter at all?

We will encounter all of these in this chapter. In section 1, we will work with advanced tuplets, exploring groupings of nine, eleven, thirteen, and fifteen. In section 2, we will work with simultaneous meters, practicing duets that use two different meters at the same time. In section 3, we will explore unmetered rhythms, like those used in recitatives, cadenzas, and freely improvised music.

21.1   Complex Tuplets

In this section, we will work with tuplet groupings larger than seven. Because there are so many notes under a single tuplet bracket, they generally spread across more than one beat. I think of these as "complex" or "advanced" tuplets. As in Chapter 19, I find it easiest to use letters of the alphabet when speaking these rhythms.

Examples A, B, and G feature groupings of nine notes in the space of two beats. Speak these rhythms using the letters A through I, with beat two falling between the "E" and the "F" as modeled below.

Complex tuplets are often indicated with a ratio, X:Y, indicating that the X durations of the tuplet fill the space generally allotted to Y notes of the same value. For example, in the "Nine Notes in Two Beats" exercise below, the tuplets in bars 3, 5, and 7 are marked with the ratio 9:8, indicating that the nine sixteenth notes in the tuplet fill the space that eight sixteenth notes generally would.

Nine Notes in Two Beats (A, B, and G)

21.1a

21.1b

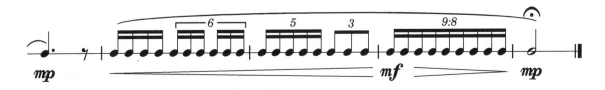

Examples C and D feature eleven-note tuplets in the space of two beats. Speak these with the letters A through K, with beat two falling between the "F" and the "G."

Eleven Notes in Two Beats

21.1c Interpret

Methodical ($\half = 56$)

21.1d Interpret

Example E features thirteen notes in the space of two beats. Use the letters A through M, with the second beat falling between the "G" and the "H."

Thirteen Notes in Two Beats

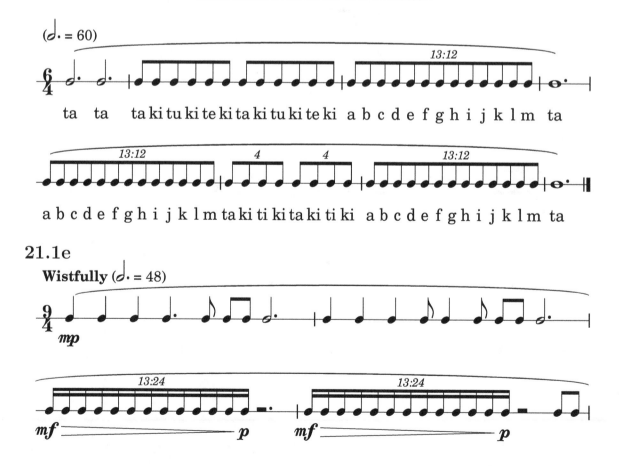

21.1e

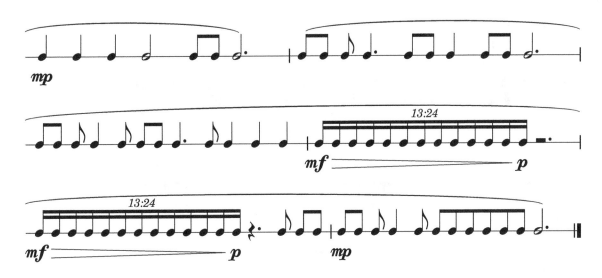

Examples F and J feature fifteen notes in the space of four beats. Use the letters A through O. Beat two will fall between the "C" and the "D," though closer to the "D." Beat three will fall evenly between the H and the I. Beat four will fall between the "L" and the "M," though closer to the "L."

Fifteen Notes in Four Beats (F and J)

21.1f

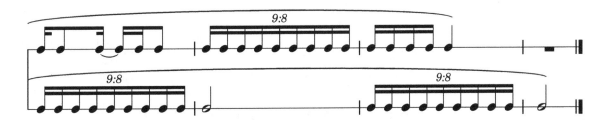

Example H features eleven notes in the space of three beats. Use the letters A through K. Beat two will fall between the "D" and the "E," though closer to the E. Beat three will fall between the "H" and the "I," though closer to the "H."

Eleven Notes in Three Beats

Example I features thirteen notes in the space of three beats. Use the letters A through M. The second beat will fall between the "E" and the "F," though closer to the "E." The third beat will fall between the "I" and the "J," though closer to the "J."

Thirteen Notes in Three Beats

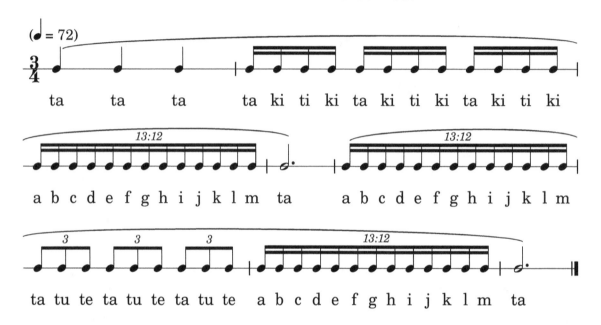

21.1i

Funky, sixteenths slightly swung (♩ = 96)

21.1j

21.2 Simultaneous Meters

Imagine that you are composing a duet for violin and cello. In the violin, the beat is consistently divided into two parts and subdivided into four parts, in the manner of simple meter. Though the beat is the same in the cello, it is consistently divided into three parts, as in compound meter. How would you notate your duet?

One approach would be to write both the violin and cello parts in simple meter and use lots of triplet brackets in the cello. Another approach would be to write both parts in compound meter, using lots of duplets and quadruplets in the violin. Though either approach would be adequate, neither is particularly elegant.

A third approach would be to notate the violin in simple meter and the cello in compound meter, indicating that the beat is the same in both parts (i.e. quarter equals 96 in the violin and dotted quarter equals 96 in the cello).

This is what we are exploring in this section: duets where each part is in a different meter. Examples A through D resemble our violin and cello scenario. One part is in simple meter and the other in compound. The beat is the same in both parts though, as the metronome marks illustrate.

These rhythms may require some extra practice. Use our standard duet process[1], with a few modifications: try counting in simple meter ("1 and 2 and...") while clapping the part in compound meter; try counting in compound meter ("1 ee uh 2 ee uh") while clapping the part in simple meter. If your three against two and three against four rhythms are at all rusty, you may want to give them a review.[2]

21.2a

---

[1]See the introduction to Chapter 3 (Semester 1).
[2]See Sections 9.2 (Semester 2) and 13.3 (Semester 3).

21.2b

21.2c Interpret

21.2d Interpret

In examples E and F, one part is in triple simple while the other is in duple compound. Here, the division of the beat and the length of the bar are the same in each part, but the beats themselves are different.

21.2e

21.2f

In examples G and H, the beats and divisions are the same in each part, but the bars are different lengths. As you practice, take turns between feeling the duet in the meter of the top part and in the meter of the bottom part.

21.2g

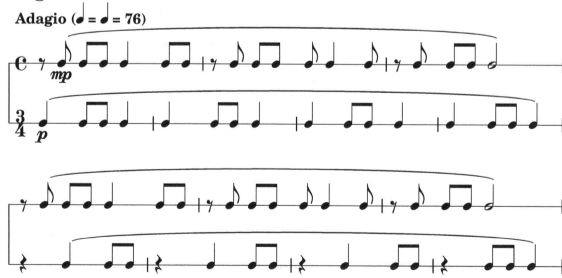

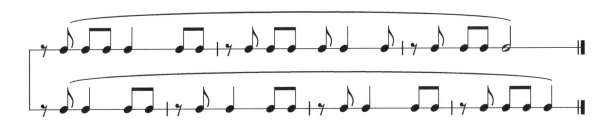

21.2h

Singsong (♩. = ♩. = 104)

In examples I and J, the beats are not the same and the bars are different lengths. The eighth note is constant in each example though. As you practice, I recommend feeling the rhythm in the meter of the top part while overlaying the shorter ostinato from the bottom part.

21.2i

21.3 Unmetered Rhythms

There are some contexts in which music is written without meter. When an improvised cadenza is notated, for example, no meter or barlines are used. Recitative passages in opera are also unmetered. So too are plainchant melodies. Modern composers may also use unmetered passages to convey a quality of timelessness or spontaneity. The examples in this section will help you gain familiarity with unmetered rhythms.

Throughout this course, we have been using rhythm syllables that are specifically linked to meter, with "ta" on the beat and "ti" or "tu te" as the division of the beat, etc. In unmetered rhythms, these syllables lose their metric context. So, be flexible. Where you see two eighths beamed together, treat them as ta-ti. Where you see three eighths beamed, use ta-tu-te. There is no one "right" way to do this, which also means that there are not, necessarily, "wrong" ways either.

21.3a

21.3c Interpret

21.3d Interpret

21.3e

21.3f

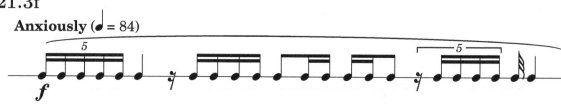

21.3g

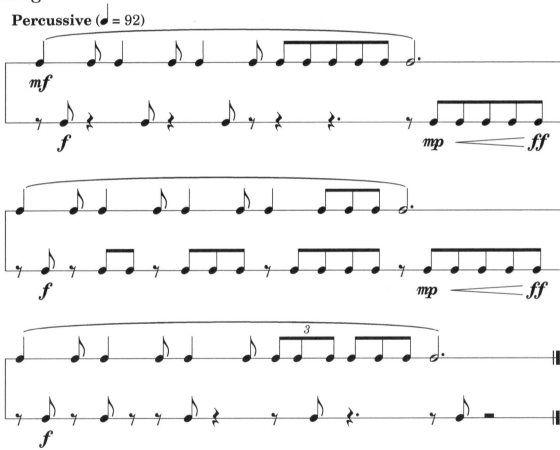

21.3h

Soporific (♩ = 66)

21.3i

Misterioso (♩ = 54)

21.3j

Playfully ($\bullet$ = 144)

Chapter 22

Symmetrical Scales

In Western music practice we use a chromatic scale with twelve notes per octave. We name these twelve notes with seven letters and represent them on the staff with seven lines and spaces. There is a certain tension here. Though the number twelve is evenly divisible by many factors, it is not evenly divisible by seven.

Since the adoption of twelve-tone equal-tempered tuning in the late eighteenth and early nineteenth centuries, the twelve half steps in the chromatic scale have been evenly spaced. Before that time, not all half steps were tuned equally. Which steps were larger and which smaller, and by how much, depended on what tuning system was being used (there were many). Consider a well-tempered harpsichord, for example. A C major scale and an F♯ major scale played on this instrument would sound different. This is not just because of the transposition; the size of the intervals in each scale would vary slightly. Equal temperament smoothed out these differences. It could very closely approximate the sound of purely-tuned major and minor scales, and do so consistently in all available transpositions.

The twelve evenly-spaced half steps of equal temperament also allowed musicians to explore new kinds of scales, scales built around the even factors of twelve (2, 4, and 6). These scales are formed from repeating patterns of small intervals. Consider dividing the octave into six groups of two half steps each. As two half steps make a whole step, this yields a scale of all whole steps known as the whole-tone scale. Consider dividing the octave into three groups of four half steps each. Now, further divide each group of four half steps into a minor third plus a half step, yielding a scale of alternating minor thirds and half steps known as the hexatonic scale. Then, divide the octave into four groups of three half steps each. Further divide each group of three half steps into a half step plus a whole step, yielding a scale of alternating half and whole steps known as the octatonic scale. As illustrated in the following vocalise, the hexatonic and octatonic scales each have two different modes, one beginning with a half step and one not.

Symmetrical Scale Vocalise

Reflecting their repeating patterns of intervals, these scales are collectively known as "symmetrical scales." There are other symmetrical scales, but these three are the most foundational. We will work with them in this chapter, exploring the whole-tone scale in section 1, the hexatonic scale in section 2, and the octatonic scale in section 3. In section 4 we will explore mixing different symmetrical scales together.

Notice that none of these scales has seven notes. The whole-tone has six notes and the hexatonic and octatonic, as their names imply, have six and eight respectively. This creates some awkwardness in rendering these scales on the staff; some scale steps will not look like steps. Notice the skip on the staff from F♯ to A♭ in the whole-tone scale above. This sounds and functions like a major second even though it is written as a diminished third. Consider too the "step" from C to C♯ in the first of the two octatonic scales shown above. This sounds and functions as a minor second, even though it is written as an augmented unison.

We are in musical territory where it serves us to flatten out some of these distinctions. In the context of this chapter, and in Chapter 24, we will think of F♯ and G♭ as being the same note — likewise with all enharmonic pairs. We will think of the minor second and the augmented unison as being the same interval — likewise with the major second/diminished third and the minor third/augmented second. Doing so will help us to understand symmetrical scales on their own terms, where the twelve-tone chromatic scale is a more useful frame of reference than are the seven-note diatonic scales of major and minor keys.

22.1   The Whole-Tone Scale

In this section we will work with the whole-tone scale. As we discussed in the introduction to this chapter, the whole-tone scale is constructed from six consecutive whole steps.

Because of their repeating patterns of intervals, symmetrical scales only have a few unique sounding transpositions.[1] The whole-tone scale on C, for example, has exactly the same set of notes as the whole-tone scale on D, E, F♯/G♭, G♯/A♭, and A♯/B♭. In fact, the whole-tone scale has only two unique transpositions. One of these includes C — we will call this "transposition 1" — and the other does not — "transposition 2."

As the sound of the whole-tone scale is likely far less familiar than that of major or minor, I recommend spending ample time with the vocalises provided. Play them at the piano to internalize their sound. Sing them through several times a day. Commit them to memory. Compose at least one similar vocalise of your own. Use my vocalises and your own as a foundation for learning the lettered examples. You should, of course, learn the lettered examples away from the piano. If you are stuck at any point, come back to the vocalises.

Notice that examples A through H, along with the vocalises, have no given key signature. If you are using movable do, treat C as do for these examples and use chromatic syllables when needed.[2]

Transposition 1

Because of the discrepancy between the six notes per octave in the whole-tone scale and the seven lines and spaces per octave on the staff, there is no single best way to write the whole-tone scale. Notice the frequent shifts between sharps and flats in the vocalises below. Negotiating these shifts will help you to be well-prepared for the melodies that follow.

The Whole-Tone Scale, Transposition 1

---

[1]Reflecting this quality, the composer Olivier Messiaen referred to symmetrical scales as "Modes of Limited Transposition."

[2]There is no solfege standard for mi sharp or ti sharp. I use "my" and "ty" here; "my" as in "mine" and "ty" as in "tie."

d te si fi m r d   d r m fi le te d   d te le fi m r d

d r m se le te d   d te le se m r d

$(\bullet\!\cdot = 76)$

d te d r d r m r m fi m fi si fi si li le te d te d r

d r d te d te le te le se si fi m fi m r m r d r d te d

$(\bullet = 66)$

d te r d m r fi m si fi li le d te r

d r te d le te se si m fi r m d r te d

$(\bullet = 66)$

d te m d fi r si m li se d le r d

d r le d se li m si r fi d m te d

22.1a

Préludes, Book 1 - No. 2, Voiles

Claude Debussy

22.1c

22.1d

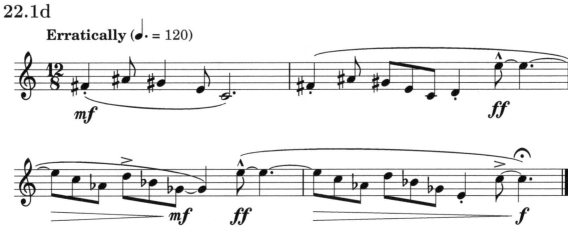

Transposition 2

The Whole-Tone Scale, Transposition 2

22.1e

22.1f

22.1g

22.1h

The Whole-Tone Scale in Major and Minor Keys

Here, we work with the whole-tone scale in the context of major and minor key signatures. Study each example to find where the whole-tone scale is used. Notice whether or not the whole-tone scale includes the tonic of the key.

If you are using movable do, try learning these examples two ways: first treating the tonic of the key as do (or la for la-based minor) and second treating C as do.

22.1i

22.1j

22.1l

22.1m

Specialty Examples

22.1n Duet

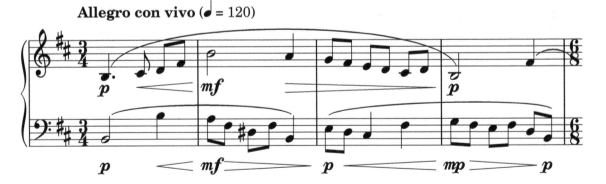

22.1o Jam Session

Misterioso (♩ = 100)
Loop indefinitely

As roman numeral analysis and figured bass are most applicable in a tonal context, I will not continue to provide these particular specialty examples in this chapter and in Chapter 24.

22.1p Lead Sheet

22.1q Find the Music

22.1r Fill in the Blanks

Listening Examples

- Classical: William Alwyn, "The Sun is Setting."

- Classical: Béla Bartók, *Mikrokosmos* Vol. V No. 136, "Whole-Tone Scales."

- Jazz: Bud Powell, "Dance of the Infidels," from *The Amazing Bud Powell (RVG Edition)* (0:00–0:48).

- Jazz: Thelonious Monk, "Four in One," from *The Genius of Modern Music Volume 2.*

- Jazz: Art Blakey and Thelonious Monk, "Blue Monk," from *Art Blakey's Jazz Messengers with Thelonious Monk* (0:00–1:21), head by Thelonious Monk. The whole-tone fragment comes in bar 10 of the blues form.

- Jazz: Lee Morgan, "Our Man Higgins," from *Cornbread* (0:00–0:50).

- Soul: Stevie Wonder, "Too High," from *Innervisions.*

22.2   The Hexatonic Scale

In this section we will work with the hexatonic scale. Just as a hexagon has six sides, the hexatonic scale has six notes per octave, arranged in a repeating pattern of minor third + half step + minor third + half step + minor third + half step.

Because of this repeating pattern, there are only two different modes of the hexatonic scale. One mode begins with a minor third. The other mode begins with a half step. The minor third mode has a major triad, a minor triad, and an augmented triad — all in root position — on its tonic. The half step mode, by contrast, only has an augmented triad on its tonic. Consequently, I think of the minor third mode as "mode 1" and the half step mode as "mode 2."

As the minor third + half step structure of the hexatonic scale repeats every four half steps — the minor third having three half steps and three plus one equaling four — there are only four unique transpositions of the hexatonic scale. We will work with all four in the examples below.

Hexatonic Mode 1

The Hexatonic Scale, Mode 1

Thirds Vocalise, Mode 1

Triads Vocalise, Mode 1

22.2a

Spunkily (♩. = 116)

22.2b

Fiery, eighth constant (♩ = 152)

22.2c

22.2d

Hexatonic Mode 2

The Hexatonic Scale, Mode 2

Three Steps Vocalise, Mode 2

Thirds Vocalise, Mode 2

Triads Vocalise, Mode 2

ri si t d le me   mes d   d s m   m s t   t si m   ri

22.2e

22.2g

22.2h

The Hexatonic Scale in Major and Minor Keys

22.2i

22.2j

22.2k

22.2l

22.2m

22.2n Duet

Specialty Examples

22.2o Jam Session

Dreamily (♩ = 72)

Cadence

22.2p Lead Sheet

22.2q Find the Music

22.2r Fill in the Blanks

Listening Examples

- Jazz: Oliver Nelson, "Stolen Moments," from *The Blues and the Abstract Truth* (4:16–5:53). The hexatonic phrase begins around the 5:29 mark.

- Jazz: Oliver Nelson, "Hoe-Down," from *The Blues and the Abstract Truth* (0:00–0:47). The bridge of this tune features the hexatonic scale in various transpositions.

22.3 The Octatonic Scale

In this section we will work with the octatonic scale. Just as an octopus has eight legs and an octagon has eight sides, the octatonic scale has eight notes per octave, arranged in a repeating pattern of half step + whole step + half step + whole step...

Because of this repeating pattern, there are only two modes of the octatonic scale. One begins with a half step and the other with a whole step. The half step mode has a major triad, a minor triad, and a diminished triad — all in root position — on its tonic. The whole step mode, by contrast, has only a diminished triad on its tonic. Consequently, I think of the half step mode as "mode 1" and the whole step mode as "mode 2."

Octatonic Mode 1

The Octatonic Scale, Mode 1

m f s le s le te de te   te de te le s le s f m f m r   di r di t   li

Thirds Vocalise, Mode 1

(♩ = 72)

d me di m ri fi m s   fi l s te l d te ra d   ra te d l te s

l fi s m fi ri m di me d ra te d   t r d me r f me se

f le fi l si t l d t   d l t si l fi le f se me f r me d

r t d l t   li di t r di m r f m s f le s te si t

li t si te s le f s m f r m di r t di li t si li

Triads Vocalise, Mode 1

22.3a

22.3b

22.3c

22.3d

Octatonic Mode 2

The Octatonic Scale, Mode 2

Thirds Vocalise, Mode 2

Triads Vocalise, Mode 2

22.3e

22.3f

22.3g

22.3h

Animato ($\bullet$ = 138)

The Octatonic Scale in Major and Minor Keys

22.3i

22.3k

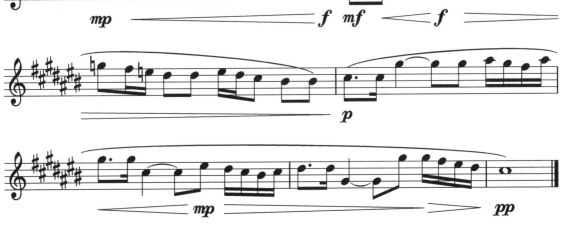

22.3m

Specialty Examples

22.3n Duet

The Rite of Spring

Igor Stravinsky

22.3o Jam Session

22.3p Lead Sheet

22.3q Find the Music

22.3r Fill in the Blanks

Listening Examples

- Classical: Béla Bartók, *Mikrokosmos* Vol. I No. 25, "Imitation and Inversion (II)."

- Classical: Béla Bartók, *Mikrokosmos* Vol. IV No. 99, "Hands Crossing."

- Classical: Béla Bartók, *Mikrokosmos* Vol. IV No. 109, "From the Island of Bali."

- Jazz: Dizzy Gillespie, Sonny Stitt, and Sonny Rollins, "The Eternal Triangle," from *Sonny Side Up* (4:10–4:22), head by Sonny Stitt. The tenor saxophone battle between Rollins and Stitt on this track is a classic. The octatonic fragment featured here comes from Stitt's solo.

- Jazz: Gary Burton, "Country Roads," from *Like Minds* (3:42–4:33). Listen to this solo by Chick Corea for examples of how the octatonic scale is mixed with other scales over a slow blues progression.

22.4   Mixing Symmetrical Scales

In this section, we will explore mixing different symmetrical scales. This is similar to our work with mode mixture in Chapter 20, only now we are mixing symmetrical scales rather than diatonic modes.

Simple Pivots

These examples combine two different symmetrical scales, staying with each for an extended period.

22.4a

22.4b

Freely Mixing Two Scales

These examples combine the notes of two different symmetrical scales, moving between them more freely and frequently.

22.4e

22.4f

22.4g

22.4h

Mixing More Scales

These examples combine three or more different symmetrical scales, sometimes pivoting between them definitively, sometimes mixing them more freely, and occasionally moving the tonic along the way.

22.4i

22.4j

22.4m

Specialty Examples

22.4n Duet

22.4o Jam Session

22.4p Lead Sheet

22.4q Find the Music

22.4r Fill in the Blanks

Jazz waltz (♩ = 112)

Listening Examples

- Classical: Béla Bartók, *Mikrokosmos* Vol. II No. 62, "Minor Sixths in Parallel Motion."

- Classical: Béla Bartók, *Mikrokosmos* Vol. IV No. 97, "Notturno."

- Classical: Béla Bartók, *Mikrokosmos* Vol. IV No. 101, "Diminished Fifth."

- Classical: Olivier Messiaen, *Quartet for the End of Time*, "Intermède."

- Television: Walter Schumann and Miklós Rózsa, theme from *Dragnet*.

Chapter 23

Metric Modulation and Advanced Polyrhythms

We have arrived at the final rhythm chapter in the course. We will be working with two high-level topics: metric modulation (sometimes known as tempo modulation) and advanced polyrhythms.

A metric modulation is a structured way of changing tempo in the middle of a piece of music. Often the meter changes at the same time, though sometimes the meter will stay constant. In either case, the listener's experience of the meter will change; hence the term metric modulation. We will work with basic metric modulations in section 1 and more complex modulations in section 2.

We have already worked with some basic polyrhythms: three against two (Chapter 9), four against three (Chapter 13), and even five and seven against two (Chapter 19). What about more complex polyrhythms, such as five against three or seven against five? We will explore these, and more combinations, in section 3.

23.1   Basic Metric Modulations

In Chapter 15, we explored changing between simple and compound meters in two different ways. First, we kept the division of the beat constant, which made for longer beats in compound meter and shorter beats in simple meter. Second, we kept the beat constant, making for shorter divisions in compound meter and longer divisions in simple meter. Examples A and B combine both of these strategies. Sometimes the division stays constant and the beat changes; sometimes the beat stays constant and the division changes. Pay attention to the metronome marks throughout each example for clues about these changes.

Sometimes composers will indicate each new tempo explicitly. Sometimes it is up to the performer to work this out independently. The math is fairly basic here, though it is easy to get confused at first.

Consider example A. The rhythm begins at 56 beats per minute. When the meter changes in bar 7, the eighth note stays constant. Before the meter change there were three eighth notes per beat. Since there had been 56 beats per minute, this means that there are 3 * 56 eighth notes per minute, or 168. Starting in bar 7, there are only two eighth notes per beat. The length of each eighth note has not changed, so each beat is 168 / 2 beats per minute, or 84. The meter changes again in bar 13. this time the beat stays constant at 84 beats per minute. The eighth notes get faster here, though, with three per beat: 3 * 84 = 252 eighths per minute. In bar 19 the meter changes again. Now the eighth note is constant (still 252 eighths per minute) with only two eighth notes per beat, so the beat is 252 / 2 or 126 beats per minute.

23.1a

23.1b

Examples C through F feature tempo changes with no change in meter. In example C, the triplet quarter note becomes the new quarter note in bar 5. In example D, the triplet eighth becomes the new sixteenth in bar 9, reverting to the original tempo in bar 13. In example E, the duplet eighth note becomes the eighth note in bar 9 and again in bar 13. In example F, the quadruplet quarter note becomes the new quarter note in bar 9 and again in bar 15.

23.1c Interpret

23.1d Interpret

23.1e

23.1f

Duets G through J feature a mixture of the techniques introduced earlier in this section. Study the metronome marks in these examples for clues about each modulation.

23.1g

23.1h

23.1i

23.2   Advanced Metric Modulations

In this section, we explore more complex ways of changing tempo and meter. Examples A and B feature modulations between meters with different pulse values, such as the move from quarter note pulse to half note pulse in bar 13 of example A.

23.2a

23.2b

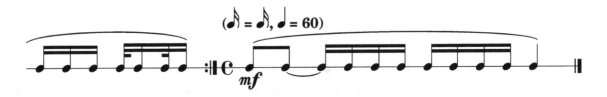

Examples C and D feature modulations with quintuplets.

23.2c Interpret

23.2d Interpret

Jaunty (♩ = 60)

Examples E and F feature modulations with composite meters.

23.2e

Exuberantly (♪. = 112)

23.2f

Duets G through J feature a mixture of the techniques introduced earlier in this section.

23.2g

23.2h

23.2i

23.2j

23.3 Advanced Polyrhythms

Each example in this section features a different polyrhythm. Before practicing the example, isolate the polyrhythm. Speak one part repeatedly with a metronome. Then clap the other part repeatedly. Continue to alternate between speaking one part and clapping the other, changing between the two more and more frequently. Then try both at the same time. Be willing to fail at this spectacularly. Keep trying. With time and repetition, the skill will come.

Our first three examples feature polyrhythms with quintuplets: five with three in example A, five with four in example B, and five with six in example C.

23.3a

Jovially (♩ = 72)

23.3b

23.3c Interpret

Our next four examples feature polyrhythms with septuplets: seven with three in example D, seven with four in example E, seven with five in example F, and seven with six in example G.

23.3d Interpret

23.3e

23.3f

23.3g

Our last three examples feature polyrhythms with groupings of eight: eight with three in example H, eight with five in example I, and eight with seven in example J.

23.3h

23.3i

23.3j

Chapter 24

Free Chromaticism

In this chapter we will explore freely chromatic melodies. We have already severed ties to seven-note diatonic scales. Here, we will sever ties with the concept of scale entirely. In place of scales, we will work with intervals as the primary building blocks of melody. This intervallic orientation is commonly known as atonality.

The term atonality was first applied to the music of Arnold Schoenberg (1874-1951), an art music composer of the Second Viennese School. It is important to emphasize that, for Schoenberg, embracing a freely chromatic landscape was not a rejection of the tonal language of the 18th and 19th centuries, with which he was deeply fluent. Indeed, he saw his work as following the innovations of tonal composers such as Mahler and Wagner to their seemingly inevitable conclusion. Schoenberg's word to describe his work was pantonality. The designation of atonality was adopted by critics of his style. Pantonality/atonality also emerged in the jazz tradition in the mid 20th century, under names such as "free," "out," and "avant-garde," with the innovations of musicians such as Cecil Taylor (1929-2018) and Ornette Coleman (1930-2015).

Studying free chromaticism has application far beyond the music of Schoenberg and the jazz avant-garde, though. It even has application beyond music of the past hundred or so years. Many tonal composers would use highly chromatic material as a means of heightening tension and drama. We will study melodies in this chapter by Tchaikovsky, Bruckner, Mahler, Respighi, and even Mozart.

I continue to encourage the use of a fixed-do system at this stage of the course. Treat C as do, using chromatic syllables for all sharps and flats. I also encourage beginning each practice session by singing various intervals up and down chromatically as modeled below. You should expand or limit these drills to best fit your vocal range. Once you master minor thirds, practice minor thirds and major thirds. Once you have mastered major thirds, add perfect fourths to your practice. Continue in this way until you are working with all intervals smaller than an octave. It is fine if your vocal range cannot support a full octave's worth of major sevenths; simply practice those that fit within your range.

As this is the last chapter of the course, and as freely chromatic music tends to be less familiar for many students, I am deviating from the structure of other melody chapters so that we can spend more time with this material. In section 1, we will discuss a theoretical framework for understanding free chromaticism; this discussion is optional and may be skipped by those eager to get to the melodies. In sections 2 through 5, we will develop the skill of navigating chromatic space intervallically, working with three-note collections known as trichords. In section 6, we will apply the skills we have developed to highly chromatic tonal melodies and to freely atonal melodies alike.

24.1 Foundations of Free Chromaticism

In studying free chromaticism, we can benefit by drawing on concepts from a branch of analysis known as set theory, which is only somewhat analogous to set theory in mathematics. In this section, we will discuss some of the foundations of musical set theory, introducing the concepts of pitch class, interval class, inversion, and set class. Please note that this discussion is far from exhaustive. I include it here to provide a context for the examples in sections 2 through 6 of this chapter.

Note and Interval Names

One of the challenges of adopting a chromatic orientation to musical space is that much of the nomenclature used in music, even at a foundational level, reflects the bias of diatonicism. For example, we use seven letters in naming notes, reflecting the prevalence of seven-note scales. Interval names such as major second and minor third also share this bias, as they refer to the number of adjacent diatonic notes contained within an interval. In light of this, some who have chosen to delve deeply into a freely chromatic landscape have adopted new systems for naming notes and intervals. C, or some other note with particular significance, may be designated as 0, other notes being numbered upwards from there by half step, with the letters "t" and "e" (or sometimes "a" and "b") being used in place of the numbers 10 and 11 to avoid double digits. For example, if C is designated as 0, D would be 2, F 5, A 9, and B e for eleven. Similarly, intervals are expressed in terms of the number of half steps they contain. For example, a major second thus becomes 2, a minor third 3, and a perfect fourth 5.[1]

Pitch Class

The concepts employed in understanding and exploring atonality are reductive in nature: they take a complex musical surface and reduce it to its simplest terms, specifically with respect to pitch. The first of these reductive concepts involves register. In this orientation, notes may be transposed by octave without impacting their basic identity. In other words, an A is an A is an A, regardless of register. The term "pitch class" is used to indicate this characteristic. For example, the pitch class A indicates any A♮ in any register, to be contrasted with the pitch A4 which refers to a specific A in a specific octave.

---

[1]For simplicity, I will continue to use conventional note and interval names throughout this chapter.

Interval Class

If we can freely transpose notes by octave without impacting their pitch class, then we can greatly simplify how we think about intervals. Consider the following process:

1. Choose any two pitch classes (for example, E♭ and C).

2. Now, play these two pitch classes at the piano so that they are as close to each other as possible. (In our example, this puts the C on the bottom with the E♭ just above it.)

3. Count the number of half steps between the two notes you are playing. If you get a number greater than six, then your pitch classes are not as close together as they could be. (In our example, this is three.)

4. Make a note of the pitch classes and the number of half steps between them (C-E♭, 3).

5. The number expresses the most basic intervallic relationship between the two pitch classes. It is the "interval class," or "ic" for short.

6. Repeat this process multiple times. How many different interval classes can you find?

Though we could express E♭ and C as a minor third, as a major sixth, minor tenth, or any number of larger intervals, the interval class between E♭ and C will always be 3. Did you notice that there are only seven different interval classes (0 through 6)? The following list shows the different interval classes and the most basic intervals that they represent.

IC 0 Perfect Unison, Perfect Octave, Perfect Fifteenth

IC 1 Minor Second, Major Seventh, Minor Ninth, Major Fourteenth

IC 2 Major Second, Minor Seventh, Major Ninth, Minor Fourteenth

IC 3 Minor Third, Major Sixth, Minor Tenth, Major Thirteenth

IC 4 Major Third, Minor Sixth, Major Tenth, Minor Thirteenth

IC 5 Perfect Fourth, Perfect Fifth, Perfect Eleventh, Perfect Twelfth

IC 6 Augmented Fourth, Diminished Fifth, Augmented Eleventh, Diminished Twelfth

Sets and Prime Form

In the language of those who study atonality, collections of pitch classes are known as sets. If pitch classes are the atoms of atonality, sets are the molecules. When written, a set is expressed within curly braces with its elements separated by commas. For example, the notes D, B, and E can be expressed as the set {D, B, E}. The order of elements in a set is insignificant, so the same group of notes could just as easily be represented as {E, D, B}, or {B, D, E}.

Just as pitches may be expressed in simplest form as pitch classes and intervals can be expressed in simplest form as interval classes, so too can sets be expressed in simplest form. But, what is the "simplest form" of a set? To answer this question, we need to first visit the concepts of inversion and transposition.

We generally use the term inversion in music to describe positions of a harmony, as in root position, first inversion, and second inversion. In atonality though, the term inversion refers to a reversing in order, from bottom to top, of the intervals contained within a set.[2] For example, the set C, D, F♯ has interval class 2 on the bottom and interval class 4 on top. An inversion of this set, {C, E, F♯} has interval class 4 on the bottom and interval class 2 on the top.

In the context of atonality, we can treat a set and its inversion as being identical in essence, like two expressions of the same blueprint.[3] Two sets also share the same blueprint if one can be transposed into the other. For example, the sets {C, D, E} and {E♭, F, G} share the same blueprint because {E♭, F, G} is simply {C, D, E} transposed up a minor third.

To summarize, the notes of a set can be expressed in any octave and in any order without altering the basic blueprint of the set. They can also be inverted and transposed without altering the basic blueprint of the set. This basic blueprint is called the "prime form" of the set. It is the distilled essence or archetype of the set, containing all of the complex relationships of the set within it.

Trichords

In sections 2 through 5 of this chapter, we will work with three-note sets in prime form, known as trichords. Use the following steps to discover as many different trichords as you can:

1. Choose any three pitch classes. For example: F♯, C, and B♭.

---

[2]To distinguish between these two uses of "inversion," I think of the inversions of a harmony as "position inversion" and the mirror image inversion of the intervals within a set as "reflection inversion."

[3]This is consistent with the work of Alan Forte, a notable writer on musical set theory. Some theorists do not equate a collection and its inversion so liberally.

2. Play these three pitch classes on the piano so that they are as close together as possible. This would put F♯ on the bottom, B♭ in the middle, and C on the top.

3. Notice the intervals/interval classes between these notes. In our example, the bottom interval is a diminished fourth (IC 4), the top interval is a major second (IC 2), and the outside interval is a diminished fifth (IC 6).

4. If the bottom interval is the smallest, then label the bottom note as "0." If the top interval is the smallest, then label the top note as 0. If the bottom and top intervals are the same size, then label either the bottom or the top note as 0, but not both. In our example, C is 0 because the smallest interval is on the top.

5. Now, assign numbers to the other notes according to how many half steps they are away from 0. (B♭ would be 2 and F♯ would be 6.)

6. Write all three numbers from smallest to largest inside square brackets. Our collection would be [026]. This is the prime form of the set {F♯, B♭, C}.

7. Repeat this process multiple times. How many different prime forms can you discover?

If you were to repeat this process indefinitely, you would only discover a dozen unique trichords. Any group of three notes can be reduced to one of these twelve prime forms: [012], [013], [014], [015], [016], [024], [025], [026], [027], [036], [037], and [048]. As it happens, we have already exhaustively explored four of these during our work with symmetrical scales: [024], [026], and [048] when working with the whole-tone scale and [036] when working with the octatonic scale. We will tackle the remaining eight in this chapter, working with two a piece in each of the next four sections.

24.2   [027] and [025]

In this and the next three sections, we will work with trichords one by one, starting with the easiest to sing and gradually progressing to the most difficult. Each trichord contains a certain group of intervals. I will point these out along the way. The melodies presented are constructed exclusively from these intervals. Take the time to practice singing each of these intervals up and down chromatically as modeled in the introduction to this chapter. Also, memorize the vocalise provided for each trichord and learn it in as many different transpositions as you can. This practice will make it much easier to learn the melodies themselves.

The [027] Trichord

The [027] trichord has an interval class 2 (0-2) and two interval class 5's (0-7 and 2-7). Warm up for these melodies by singing major seconds, perfect fourths, perfect fifths, and minor sevenths.

[027] Vocalise

24.2a

24.2b

24.2c

24.2d

The [025] Trichord

The [025] trichord has an interval class 2 (0-2), an interval class 3 (2-5), and an interval class 5 (0-5). Warm up for these melodies by practicing major seconds, minor thirds, perfect fourths, perfect fifths, major sixths, and minor sevenths.

[025] Vocalise

24.2e

24.2f

24.2g

24.2h

Specialty Examples

24.2i Duet

24.2j Jam Session

24.2k Lead Sheet

24.2l Find the Music

24.2m Fill in the Blanks

24.3   [037] and [015]

The [037] Trichord

The [037] trichord has an interval class 3 (0-3), an interval class 4 (3-7), and an interval class 5 (0-7). Warm up for these melodies by singing minor thirds, major thirds, perfect fourths, perfect fifths, minor sixths, and major sixths.

[037] Vocalise

24.3a

The [015] Trichord

The [015] trichord has an interval class 1 (0-1), an interval class 4 (1-5), and an interval class 5 (0-5). Warm up for these melodies by singing minor seconds, major thirds, perfect fourths, perfect fifths, minor sixths, and major sevenths.

[015] Vocalise

24.3e

24.3f

24.3g

24.3h

Specialty Examples

24.3i Duet

24.3j Jam Session

24.3k Lead Sheet

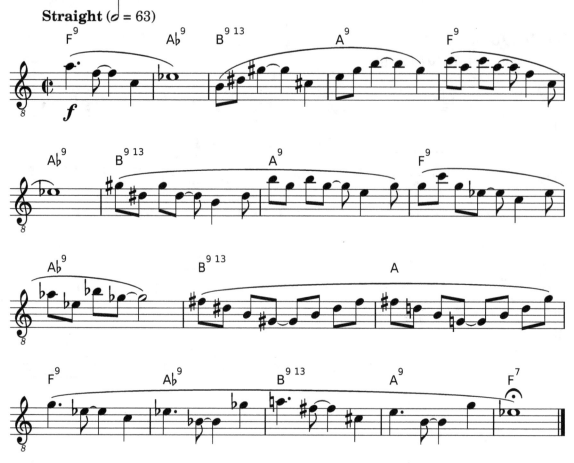

24.3l Find the Music

24.3m Fill in the Blanks

Ambulatory (♩ = 76)

24.4   [013] and [014]

The [013] Trichord

The [013] trichord has an interval class 1 (0-1), an interval class 2 (1-3), and an interval class 3 (0-3). Warm up for these melodies by singing minor seconds, major seconds, minor thirds, major sixths, minor sevenths, and major sevenths.

[013] Vocalise

24.4a

Bewildered (♩ = 84)

24.4b

24.4c

24.4d

The [014] Trichord

The [014] trichord has an interval class 1 (0-1), an interval class 3 (1-4), and an interval class 4 (0-4). Warm up for these melodies by singing minor seconds, minor thirds, major thirds, minor sixths, major sixths, and major sevenths.

[014] Vocalise

24.4e

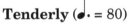

Tenderly (♩. = 80)

24.4f

Tribute to Darth Vadar (♩. = 112)

24.4g

Specialty Examples

24.4i Duet

Sostenuto (♩. = 63)

24.4j Jam Session

24.4k Lead Sheet

24.4l Find the Music

24.4m Fill in the Blanks

24.5   [016] and [012]

The [016] Trichord

The [016] trichord has an interval class 1 (0-1), an interval class 5 (1-6), and an interval class 6 (0-6). Warm up for these melodies by singing minor seconds, perfect fourths, augmented fourths, diminished fifths, perfect fifths, and major sevenths.

[016] Vocalise

24.5a

24.5b

24.5d

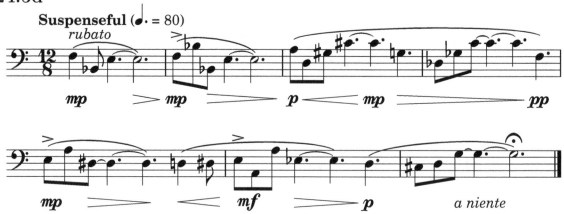

The [012] Trichord

The [012] trichord has two interval class 1's (0-1 and 1-2), and an interval class 2 (0-2). Warm up for these melodies by singing minor seconds, major seconds, minor sevenths, and major sevenths.

[012] Vocalise

24.5e

24.5f

24.5g

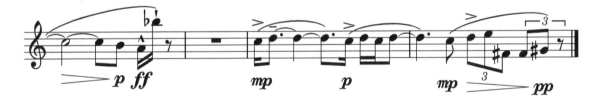

24.5h

Specialty Examples

24.5i Duet

24.5j Jam Session

24.5k Lead Sheet

24.5l Find the Music

24.5m Fill in the Blanks

24.6   Applying Chromatic Materials

Now that we have systematically worked with each trichord and its corresponding intervals in turn, it is time to work with freely chromatic melodies. We will start with chromatic melodies written with key signatures. Though it would be possible to approach these melodies from a movable do perspective, stay with fixed do here and orient intervallically.

Examples in Major Keys

24.6a

Symphony No. 5 in B-flat major

Anton Bruckner

24.6b

Symphony No. 10

Gustav Mahler

24.6c

Rhapsody for Orchestra and Saxophone

Claude Debussy

24.6d

Le triomphe de Bacchus

Claude Debussy

Examples in Minor Keys

24.6e

The Firebird

Igor Stravinsky

24.6f

Prelude to the Afternoon of a Faun

Claude Debussy

24.6g

Sei Melodie - No. 1, In alto mare

Ottorino Respighi

24.6h

Piano Concert No. 1 in B-flat minor, Op. 23

Pyotr Tchaikovsky

Examples without Key Signatures

24.6i

24.6j

3 Pieces, Op. 11 - No. 1 - Mässige Viertel

Arnold Schoenberg

24.6k

24.6l

2 Elegies, First Elegy

Béla Bartók

24.6m

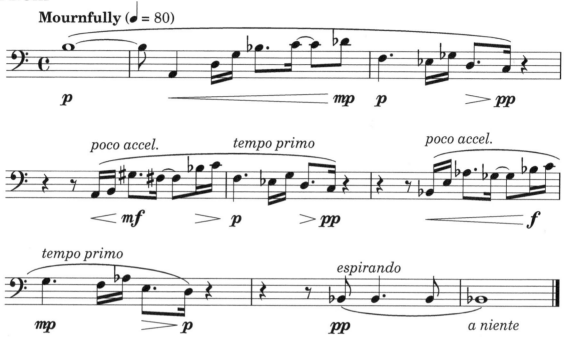

Tone Rows

Examples N through R are not melodies at all, but tone rows. Each presents an arrangement of the twelve notes of the chromatic scale in a particular sequence. Try some of the following activities with these examples:

- Sing the row through from left to right.

- Sing the row in retrograde, reading from right to left.

- Repeat the row several times, improvising rhythms and phrases as you go. As you become more comfortable with this, play with dynamics and articulations as well.

- Repeat the row several times, improvising rhythms and phrases as above. Play with repeating individual notes or groups of notes as often as you wish.

- Sing the row, transposing one or two notes up or down by octave.

- Write out the row in several different transpositions (up a minor third, down a whole step, etc.). Sing through these transpositions, keeping C as do.

- Memorize the sequence of intervals in the row and try transposing it "on the fly."

24.6n

24.6o

24.6p

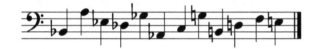

24.6q

24.6r

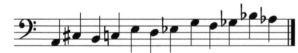

Listening Examples

- Classical: Wolfgang Amadeus Mozart, Symphony No. 40 in G Minor fourth movement, K. 550. Listen to the first four bars of the development section.

- Musical Theater: George Gershwin, "Bess, You Is My Woman Now," from *Porgy and Bess* (original cast recording, 0:20–1:16).

- Classical: Béla Bartók, *Mikrokosmos* Vol. II No. 54, "Chromatics."

- Classical: Béla Bartók, *Mikrokosmos* Vol. II No. 64, "Line Against Point."

- Classical: Béla Bartók, *Mikrokosmos* Vol. III No. 80, "Hommage à Robert Schumann."

- Classical: Béla Bartók, *Mikrokosmos* Vol. IV No. 105, "Game (with Two Five-Tone Scales)."

- Classical: Olivier Messiaen, *Quartet for the End of Time*, "Danse de la fureur, pour les sept trompettes."

- Television: Alexander Courage, theme from *Star Trek*. In the beginning, follow the notes as the instruments enter one at a time. When the voice comes in, follow that.

- Musical Theater: Leonard Bernstein, "Glitter and be Gay," from *Candide* (original cast recording, 0:10–0:42).

- Jazz: Chick Corea, "Matrix," from *Now He Sings, Now He Sobs* (0:00–0:21).

- Folk: Joni Mitchell, "Songs to Aging Children Come," from *Clouds*.

- Pop: Barbra Streisand, "I'm All Smiles," from *People*, written by Michael Leonard and Herbert Martin.

- Jazz: Michael Brecker, "Syzygy," from *Michael Brecker*.

- Jazz Fusion: Pat Metheny Group, "The Heat of the Day," from *Imaginary Day* (2:13–2:37), written by Pat Metheny and Lyle Mays.

- Video Games: Koji Kondo, "Super Mario Bros," performed by The London Philharmonic Orchestra, from *The Greatest Video Game Music* (2:37–3:05). Don't worry so much about rhythmic accuracy here; this arrangement takes some liberties with the rhythm. Nonetheless, enjoy the ominous atonality of this classic theme.

- Video Games: Kaveh Cohen and Michael David Nielsen, "Splinter Cell: Conviction," performed by The London Philharmonic Orchestra, from *The Greatest Video Game Music* (0:54–1:15).

- Video Games: Masashi Hamauzu, "Final Fantasy XIII: Hanging Edge," performed by The London Philharmonic Orchestra, from *The Greatest Video Game Music* (0:00–0:44). Learn the duet between the piano melody and the string part that comes in half way through. Each part by itself is highly modal. The two together are strikingly bitonal.

CPSIA information can be obtained
at www.ICGtesting.com
Printed in the USA
LVHW010818030121
675538LV00009BA/1074